The
Sexual
Novice

Taking Those
First Steps

Robert W. Birch, Ph.D.
ACS Certified Sexologist

THE SEXUAL NOVICE:
Taking Those First Steps

By Robert W. Birch, Ph.D.

Published in the United States

ISBN-10 =1453702288
ISBN-13 =9781453702284

PEC Publishing
429 Grand Ridge Dr.
Howard, OH 43028

http://www.oralcaress.com

For all those who have been waiting and wondering and those now wanting to take those next steps.

Table of Contents

Virginity:

When you have it
&
When you don't!

Defining virginity and the loss thereof is not simple, as there are physical, spiritual, and personal definitions of the word. The physical definition says that if the internal tissue, known as the hymen, is torn, the woman is no longer a virgin. Historically it was the presence of an intact hymen that was considered the mark of virginity. If a woman has used an insertable vibrator or dildo, and her toy has torn or stretched her hymen, she has, by the physical definition, "lost her cherry." The problem with this definitions is, of course, that physical activity of almost any sort, the use of penetrating fingers during self-stimulation or sex play, a medical pelvic exam, or the use of tampons can tear the hymen long before a penis is ever inserted. By this definition, a woman could lose her virginity alone and through nonsexual activity.

It is the religious concept that causes most people to experience guilt and shame, as the word purity becomes associated with virginity. The theological loss of virginity occurs when the woman has her first intercourse, but the premarital sin is not specific as to depth or duration, or the love shared (or not shared) by the couple. Historically, this prohibition was probably associated with viewing intercourse as being only for the purpose of procreation, rather than recreation. Before the relatively recent introduction of birth control techniques, saving intercourse for marriage might well have been the church's attempt to prevent children from being born out of wedlock and thus having to grow up without a father. This moratorium on premarital intercourse is so much a part of our society, that the definition is accepted even by those who are not religious, although ignored by many who are. By this definition, a woman can lose her virginity without feeling passion, pleasure or orgasm. The physical act is the "sin," not the intent, the feelings, or the outcome.

The personal definition is quite flexible. If a woman feels she is a virgin until she has intercourse with a man she loves, she can give herself permission to have a number of casual affairs, and still feel justified in wearing white (the symbol of purity) on her wedding day. If another woman feels she will forfeit her purity if a man arouses her, she will avoid sexual stimulation.

I should also add the neighbors' definition. There was a time when bed sheets were displayed outside after the wedding night, so that neighbors could observe the blood spots. No doubt in many cases the spots were from a pin prick on a finger, rather than from a ruptured hymen, but the significance of faking virginity is noteworthy. Many young girls, feeling shameful, will deny having had intercourse even to their closets friends. What neighbors think can have little similarity to the reality of the woman's hymen.

The avoidance of sex is often a matter of wording. Since in our society we have mistakenly equated the words sex and intercourse, and use them interchangeably, there are those who will do all manner of sexual activities short of copulation, but deny having sex. Clearly, "having sex" includes "having intercourse," but is not limited to it. By manipulating our vocabulary, we can give ourselves all kinds of excuses and permission!

The bottom line is not about the concepts of "virginity," but about the making of responsible decisions, about a woman's right to choose, and about maintaining self-respect regardless of the choices made. For some women the choice is to save intercourse for someone special or for marriage, but to experience the pleasures of orgasm with manual, oral or vibrator stimulation. Each woman must clarify her own set of values and decide her own limits.

First Time:

Loss of Virginity
Your Introduction to Intercourse

It will be best to start by stating the obvious -- women have been having intercourse ever since males have been getting erections and then figured out what to do with them. Every nonvirginal woman has had her first time, and 99.99% of them survived it well enough to do it again, and again, and again! Even though only about 35% of all orgasmic women are having orgasms during intercourse, most all women enjoy the act's physical and emotion closeness.

The reasons for an adult woman to maintain her virginity are numerous -- you know them. There are those who abstain for moral or religious reasons, and there are those who avoid penetration out of fear (of pain, pregnancy, disease, loss of reputation, or loss of self-respect). There are women who postpone intercourse not out of choice, but because they have not found a man they can trust, or love, or who turns them on. Some women have not had the opportunity. The woman who remains a virgin after graduating from high school probably does so for one or more of the reasons above.

When to give up ones virginity, and with whom, is every woman's choice. Unfortunately, all too many women have suffered forced penetration against their will, and a history of sexual trauma is another reason why some women might avoid consensual intercourse. With or without a history of abuse (childhood or adult), some women feel threatened by an erect penis. Too often it is seen as a potential instrument of pain, pregnancy, or humiliation. Some women see it as 'dirty,' possibly ugly, or a potential source of a sexually transmitted disease. For a lot of reasons, a lot of adult women just say "No!" That is a woman's right!

A good reason not to lose ones virginity -- the male insistence on it as a condition for continuing the relationship. A woman should not allow herself to be manipulated into it, lest she look back on the event with regret. "If you love me, you'll give it to me," or "If you don't give it to me, I'll get it somewhere else" is manipulative emotional blackmail.

There may be some reason for concern if a woman has been actively avoiding intercourse for several reasons, including the fear of pain (emotional or physical). The consequence might be the development of a cycle of avoidance. If the approach to her vaginal opening (or even her genitals) stirs intense anxiety, a woman might find that avoiding that potential penetration relieves her of that fear. In a sense, then, the avoidance reinforces or rewards itself. Essentially the woman says to herself, "I think I will, but oh my, it will be scary. I better try, but this is so frightening. Maybe it will not hurt, but I'm afraid it will. He wants to enter me, but it will not work. I want to avoid and escape, and then I will no longer feel threatened and scared. It is so nice not to have to worry about it!" Avoidance becomes the escape from fear, and fear perpetuates the avoidance. Breaking this cycle of avoidance might not be easy.

Let's shift gears for a moment and talk anatomy. There is a sling of muscles, called the pubococcygeus (pronounced pew-bo-cox-se-gee'-us) muscles, that stretches between the legs of both men and women. These muscles attach in front to the pubic bone, pass between the legs and attach to the tail or coccyx bone in back. The muscles are most commonly referred to simply as the PC Muscles.

These PC muscles, as they make their way from front to back, surround the opening of the bladder, surround the first inch or so at the opening to the vaginal canal, and form the anal sphincter, before attaching again to the tail bone. In fact, if we had tails we would use our PC muscles to wag them. When a man wiggles his penis, he is using these muscles. A woman can find her PC muscles by stopping her flow of urine. When both men and women orgasm, it is these pelvic floor PC muscles that contract, sending waves of pleasure throughout the body.

The Kegel Exercises, that strengthen the PC muscles, are taught to women wishing to learn how to orgasm, and they are taught to women who lose urine when they laugh, cough, or sneeze (urinary stress incontinence). They are also taught to new mothers to help tone up vaginal muscles that have been stretched during childbirth. So, why do I mention them in an article on first intercourse? Because if a woman is figuratively "up tight" about penetration, she might also be "up tight" literally. Anxiety about vaginal entry can translate into physical tightening of that entryway. Later we will talk of ways to relax these important muscles, but obviously to gain control, a woman must learn how.

The lost of virginity does not always occur on the soft mattress of the honeymoon bed. A lot of half-dressed young women, in the heat of passion, lose their virginity in a near impossible position in the back seat of a car. Young women are initiated into intercourse on the couch in a family room, on a park bench, or while standing in a swimming pool. For some, the loss of virginity has been easy, loosening up both emotionally and physically with, in some cases, the consumption of alcohol as the "sexual lubricant." Perhaps the first penetration is experienced as an uncomfortable, unfamiliar feeling, more than it is perceived as pain.

Typically the woman's hymen has already been torn or stretched prior to intercourse, the result of a physically active life style, the use of tampons, or a gynecologic pelvic exam. Modern women rarely have their "cherries busted," and there is not likely to be the proverbial bloodstained sheet.

For most women their first intercourse is relatively easy once they have decided (often impulsively in the midst of hot love making) to do it and if they can relax. If unmarried there might be a tinge of lingering guilt, a bit of regret the next morning, or a haunting fear of pregnancy . . . but it is over, done, and life goes on. Women do have unwanted pregnancies and get exotic sexually transmitted diseases, but for the most part the only consequences for the newly initiated are a few drops of bright red blood and a dull ache to remind her for a few days of her passageway into a new phase of her life.

There are some women, however, who are very up tight about losing their virginity, but are approaching a time when they know they must take the big step. Perhaps it is a pending marriage with apprehension about the wedding night. Perhaps it is a certain man who is extra special, or perhaps it is simply the awareness that time is passing and something is being missed.

As has been stated, if a woman is fearful of penetration and has been actively avoiding it for years, she is likely to unconsciously tighten her vaginal muscles. It is as though her body is saying, "Oh no, you are not going to get in there." One of the first steps in learning to relax a muscle is to find it, and the best way to find the PC muscles is while urinating. The muscles that are squeezed to stop the flow are the PC muscles. If the woman is orgasmic, she will recognize them as being involved in her experience of climax. Some women in trying to squeeze these muscles tighten their abdominal or thigh muscles. These muscles should stay relaxed as she locates and squeezes her pelvic floor muscles. Once identified and the woman can consciously tighten them, she can now begin to consciously learn to relax them as well. The reader should refer to the instructions for doing the Kegel Exercises.

If the woman is in an ongoing relationship, her partner plays an important role in preparing her. If he is impatient, demanding, and insensitive to her anxiety and her anticipated or real pain, the going is likely to be tough. However, if he is patient, loving and respectful, the process can go smoothly. Over repeated petting sessions, the woman can become comfortable with having her external genitalia stroked. She must be able to trust that no unannounced penetration will be attempted. Gradually, and with much talk and only when she is highly aroused, a small finger can be introduced into her vagina. This should assure her that she can, in fact, be entered. Without rushing and without hard pushing, the longer middle finger can be used, inserted slowly with the palm up as the woman lays on her back focusing on her relaxation. As a part of this introductory phase, a woman can insert tampons and even her own finger while self-pleasuring. Penetration by a penis should not occur until the woman is comfortable with finger play.

Some women, in preparation for intercourse or to "stay in shape" after a brief introduction, will use dildos . . . and, of course, they do feel good especially when combined with clitoral stimulation. I highly recommend flexible "user friendly" dildos beginning with the smaller sizes available.

Clearly, erections are larger than fingers and usually larger than the smallest dildo. If the size of a penis worries a woman, it will help if she spends time sitting on her partner, but with the shaft of his penis between the lips of her genitals. This has been called *outercourse*, and as the woman slides along the shaft of her partner's erect penis, it can be quite pleasurable to both. Once more it is important for the woman to trust that there will be no unannounced nonconsensual attempt at penetration, and one of the nice things about this position (besides feeling good) is that the woman can maintain control.

Penetration can be attempted with the woman on top, lifting up from her partner's penis and then reaching down to guide it to the opening of her vagina. She can then lower herself, stopping if she feels discomfort. The advantage to this position is her ability to control the speed and the depth of the penetration. The disadvantage is that she must support herself and this might make it difficult for her to relax. I would suggest that the first entry be made as the woman lies on her back with legs spread.

Penis size might matter initially. When being introduced to intercourse, bigger is not likely to be better. However, be assured that most men are average and most women learn to adjust to their partner, regardless of how them might be endowed. Do remember that the size of an erection does not determine if a woman will orgasm with intercourse or not. As the old saying goes, "It is not the size of the tool, but how well the man can use it."

Arousal is essential. As a woman becomes aroused, her vaginal muscles will naturally relax a bit . . . the vagina will actually open up along its entire length. The cervix usually dips down into the end of the vaginal canal. During arousal, the uterus pulls up, lifting the cervix out of the "line of fire," so that the thrusting penis will pass under it, rather than ramming into it. In addition, arousal provides the lubricant that will facilitate the insertion. I would certainly recommend adding a bit of extra lubrication the first couple times, just to be sure, but remember, no amount of artificial lubrication will make up for the lack of arousal. Arousal is nature's way of preparing the woman, and that will not come out of a tube. A woman's natural lubrication is not only superbly slippery, it is of erotically pleasing aroma and taste.

For additional lubrication I recommend a safe water-soluble sexual lubricant. Unfortunately, artificial lubrication placed outside the vagina or on the man's penis is likely to be squeegeed off as he slides through the tight virginal opening. Added lubrication that has been push back around the man's testicles does little for the woman! Gentle finger play can work some of the lubrication into the opening, but remember, an artificial product will never replace the natural lubrication of a highly aroused woman. Not highly aroused? It might be the result of high anxiety or an inability to relax. It also could be because it is the wrong time or the wrong man!

As with any intercourse with a relative stranger, first intercourse with someone of unknown history should always require the use of a condom! Better safe than sorry. It is usually best to begin with someone you know, trust and care for, but contraception should always be of high priority.

Developing a positive attitude about intercourse is important. It is fun, it is loving, it is intimate and a lot of people spend a lot of time doing it. Positive anticipation of the first time and having the right mind-set might help. The novice should develop erotic fantasies to help get into the mood and to help stay focused on the sexual excitement, rather than the sexual fear. Read the chapter on using sexual fantasy.

If the woman is very aroused but does not feel relaxed, here is something that should help. On her back, the woman should relax as much as possible. In fact, I would strongly suggest a full body erotic massage prior to attempting penetration. Once relaxed, the man should hold the end of his erection right at the opening, without attempting to push in. At this point the woman should squeeze those PC muscles tight and hold them. These muscles are such that if a woman consciously squeezes them and tries to hold them tight, they will automatically release and begin to relax. So, the woman squeezes, holds, and then allows them to relax. She should do this again . . . squeeze, hold, and relax. Then a third time . . . squeeze, hold, hold, hold . . . then a deep breath as she begins to relax and, when ready, her words "Now, gently my love."

The initial penetration should be slow and partial. If it begins to hurt, the woman should say so and, without the man pulling out, she should once more squeeze, hold, and relax. If this helps, he can then slide in a bit deeper. If her discomfort continues, he should pull out. Rome was not built in a day. Not all virgins are totally "deflowered" on first partial penetration. The man should not expect to be able to thrust deeply and rapidly during the first couple encounters. If his goal is to ejaculate in her, he does not understand her discomfort and her need to learn to relax.

Some women do experience chronic pain with intercourse, and some develop a condition known as *Vaginismus*, a psychosomatic condition that makes penetration impossible. This is the result of an automatic reaction similar to an eye blink. The muscles at the vaginal opening contract, tightening and already tight entrance. This makes penetration even more difficult and, therefore, more painful. A unconscious cycle can begin. Fear of pain might then begin to contribute to it. The key to avoiding vagnismus is total relaxation and a very patient partner..

Realistically, the vast majority of women do fairly well

with their first encounter and with each subsequent episodes of intercourse learn to relax and enjoy this special bonding. Intercourse is about mutual pleasure . . . it is about profound intimacy, and most of all it is about having fun.

One reader wrote:

I had intercourse for the first time on my wedding night when I was 26. I was excited, eager, but very wide-eyed. My husband had told me he had had intercourse two times (with the same woman) in his past. So he was relatively inexperienced. I brought KY jelly with me on the advice of a friend. We slow-danced as we undressed each other over a period of about 30 minutes, also drinking a glass of wine. We played around with each other in the bed for about 30 minutes more.

When the time drew near I applied the KY and my husband proceeded to come into me (I was on my back). After a couple of stabs he entered into me and stopped there (I had squeezed his arm as a signal to slow/stop). It felt tight and a little rough. After a minute I asked him to go a little deeper. He did and began to thrust until he climaxed about 5 minutes later. I felt no sexual sensations, but was thrilled to be finally "doing it." After three days and five times, I admitted that I was sore and needed a break!

After two weeks of marriage and frequent sex, I was well-lubed for intercourse, but did not have an orgasm (except for my own manual stimulation during foreplay) until about 9 months later.

That's it! Hope this helps someone.

The Kegel Exercises

A LITTLE HISTORY

A band of muscles stretch between the legs of both men and women, stretching from the pubic bone in front to the coccyx (tail) bone in back. Playfully, we could say that with out these muscles, all of our internal organs would fall out! Along their way, this sling of muscles includes the sphincter of the bladder, the sphincter of the anus, and, in a woman, the sphincter surround the opening of her vagina. These muscles are clinically known as the pubococcygeus (pronounced pew-bo-kak-se-gee'-us) muscles, but this group of muscles is more commonly called the "PC muscle." To talk as though there is just one muscle is an over-simplification, for there are actually a number of muscle groups that collectively make up this pelvic floor sling. We'll use the plural and call them the PC muscles.

Many younger women have been introduced to their PC muscles during a pregnancy or during a postpartum exam when they were advised to exercise these muscles in order to restore muscle tone following childbirth. Many older women have been introduced to their PC muscles because these are the muscles that are exercised to correct the condition known as urinary incontinence (the involuntary loss of urine when coughing, sneezing, etc.). In fact, the exercise of these PC muscles as a medical treatment for urinary incontinence was first proposed in1950 by the surgeon Arnold Kegel, for whom the exercises have been named.

In 1952, Dr. Kegel published a report in which he claimed that the women doing his exercises were becoming more easily, more frequently and more intensely orgasmic! As these are the muscles that contract rhythmically during orgasm in both males and females, it is not surprising, therefore, that sex therapists have emphasized the importance of these pelvic floor muscles that surround the vaginal opening and play a major role in the orgasmic response.

Thirty years after Dr. Kegel's article, sex therapist Bryce Britton wrote a book titled "THE LOVE MUSCLE," calling her publication "Every Woman's Guide to Intensifying Sexual Pleasure." Many people still refer to the PC muscles as the love muscle. Now, almost 50 years after Dr. Kegel published his discovery, and after several decades of "prescribing" the Kegel exercises as a component in teaching women to become orgasmic (or more easily orgasmic), what can we say about "Kegeling" the love muscle? We can say that doing the exercises will tone up the sphincter of the bladder and might tighten the muscles around the opening of the vagina. We can also assume that any well-toned muscle will contract more powerfully than would a flabby muscle, and hence the likelihood of stronger orgasms with stronger PC muscles. We can report with confidence that some women squeeze their PC muscles, forcing blood down into their genital tissue, and in so doing turn themselves on. A very small minority of women might even be able to bring themselves to orgasm exclusively with voluntary pelvic floor contractions. Finally, it is safe to say that a woman can add novelty to a sexual encounter by voluntarily squeezing her well-toned vaginal sphincter around her partner's penis, and this might be fun for both giver and receiver.

What can most confidently be said about the entire "PC muscle controversy" is that in doing Dr. Kegel's exercises, a woman will achieve closer contact with her pelvis, is more likely to take ownership of her internal and external genitalia, will strengthen the muscles that contract during orgasm, and is probably making an investment in her lifelong urinary control! Being in touch with these muscles will allow a woman greater ability not only to tighter her vaginal opening, but to loosen it. Thus, it can be helpful for virgins to practice the Kegel exercies. Is it a major component in a woman becoming orgasmic? Probably not, but it is certainly something non-orgasmic women should include in their quest for the "Big O." It is a part of the learning package.

DOING THE KEGEL EXERCISES

In getting started with the Kegel exercise of the PC muscles, the first task for many women is to locate them. The best advice for finding the muscles is to do so while urinating. Sitting on the toilet with legs slightly spread, try to interrupt the flow of urine without bringing your legs together. Stop and start the flow, trying to sense those muscles that are involved. Once you can control the flow of your urine and can also find and squeeze them when not on the toilet, you have identified this band of important pelvic floor muscles.

Remember, these muscles are not located in your abdomen, nor are they in your thighs! Try to isolate the muscles so you can tighten them without flexing your "abs" and without putting tension in your legs. It might take time to fine-tune your ability to find, isolate and contract the muscles, so do not become discouraged if you have difficulty at first.

Once you know you have found your PC muscles, you will find that you can flex them ("Kegeling") most any time you choose and without being noticed by others who might be around you. Doing a series of Kegel exercises each day in the course of typical activities is most helpful. For women who drive or ride to and from work each day, a practical plan is to do a series of contractions at each red light encountered, or at each gas station passed, or in response to some other reminder. While watching TV, squeeze your PC muscles during each commercial. Contract the muscles and hold them tight for a slow count to five. At first you might not make it to five, but keep trying. As with any muscle, the more you exercise that muscle, the less effort is required to tighten it and the longer you will be able to keep them tight.

In addition to taking advantage of opportunities in your daily life, set aside specific times when you can be alone at home. Lay down and relax. Starting with a warm bath might help. In your mind, find those PC muscles. Then begin tightening and relaxing five times, each time holding the contraction for a slow count of five. Your goal over a period of time is to increase the number of contractions and the length of time held (although there is a limit to which the PC muscles can be tightened before they automatically begin to relax). Work at it, each time striving to improve your count. If the muscles feel tired, stop and relax for a few seconds and then start in again.

While on your back, also try to do a series of quick Kegels, tightening and relaxing the PC muscles as rapidly as possible, initially five times. Relax for a minute and then do another series of these quick rapid contractions. Work to increase the number of contractions in each series, and work to increase the number of series. You might think of this as "fluttering" your PC muscles. Rest when you need to.

It is important to exercise often and it is helpful to add a variety of physical positions. It has also been suggested that it would be helpful to pull in the entire pelvic floor, imagining that you are able to draw water up into your vagina. Then bear down as though you are pushing this imaginary water out. Do that five times to start, and more often as you gain strength.

Initially you might want to do the exercises clothed (certainly those series performed on your way to work). At home, however, when you will be comfortable and will have the time, it might be helpful to begin doing the exercises nude. Combine your "Kegeling" with other activities designed to increase body awareness and sexual sensitivity. You might find that doing your Kegels while masturbating increases the level of your arousal and might even trigger an orgasm.

KEGELING WITH YOUR PARTNER

With a partner present and with sufficient arousal and lubrication, have your partner insert two fingers into your vagina. Once inside, your partner should open the fingers up like scissors, and you try to close them with your vaginal sphincter muscles. Repeat this five times on each occasion that you do it. If you are uncomfortable with two fingers, have your partner put in just one and then curl this finger upward. You try to straighten it out!

If you are a heterosexual woman with a partner, you might also want to use the PC muscles that surround the opening of your vaginal during intercourse. Grip and relax, grip and relax five times, saying nothing to see if your partner will acknowledge feeling you tighten around him. You could think of it as a flirtatious "vaginal wink." Have fun learning about your pubococcygeus muscles and share!!

Why a Sexual Lubricant?
SLIPPERY WAYS TO ENHANCE LOVEMAKING

One thing both men and women will learn is that good sex is wet! As a woman becomes sexually aroused, the tissue lining the first inch or so of her vagina begins to swell. As this area swells, it begins squeezing that exquisite slippery fluid (clinically called the "transudate") out through the hundreds of small ducts buried in that lining. These vaginal juices first appear right inside the vagina, and it is only as the woman's arousal builds that the sexual secretions will run out the opening, and even then there might not be any lubrication around her sensitive clitoris unless she or her partner capture some and bring it up to caress this pleasure bud. Remember, even an aroused woman might have a dry clitoris, and rubbing a dry clitoris will often produce discomfort before it creates arousal. Remember also that the majority women need clitoral stimulation in order to reach orgasm. Beginners often make the mistake of relying on intercourse to totally satisfy a woman.

It was once said that sex is perfectly natural, but unfortunately it's not naturally perfect. Under perfect conditions a highly aroused young woman will lubricate profusely, at least if she is not nursing. In reality, however, certain medications (including some over-the-counter antihistamines), pregnancy and lactation, menopause or monthly hormonal fluctuations will inhibit the production of these wonderfully slippery juices. Also, some women are just slow starters, either because of their biology or the ineptness of their lover. Anxiety can get in the way and other women might feel highly aroused but for some unknown reason remain bone dry.

I should begin with a precaution. A lover should never poke a finger, a dildo or a cylindrical vibrator into a dry vagina! Men should remember the formula: Men get hard, Women get wet! A dry vagina is an indication that arousal is incomplete. This is the time someone should grab the lubricant and apply a small amount around the woman's clitoris. A gentle massage with a slippery finger might arouse the woman and no additional lubricant, other then the woman's own, would then be needed. This works very well with slow starters and provides a wonderful learning opportunity for a man who has not learned of the importance of a woman's clitoris. Remember, the clitoris is typically the source of a woman's pleasure, not her vagina.

A woman who feels aroused, but for some reason does not sufficiently lubricate, will appreciate the application of a healthy amount of artificial lubricant not only around her clitoris, but around the opening of her vagina as well. The lubricant should be gently, but playfully, worked into the vaginal opening with a finger before a toy or penis is inserted. In fact, additional lubrication should be applied to the object, animate or inanimate, that is about to take the plunge. A good rule of thumb is that it is better to use too much lubrication than not enough.

We have talked so far about lubricants for vaginal intercourse or the insertion of toys for vaginal pleasure. However, there is another class of lubricants made specifically for anal play. One must remember that a vagina is self-lubricating, the anus is not! A lubricant must be used for safe and pleasurable anal penetration, but one must never insert a toy that could escape from slippery fingers and slide completely into the rectum! Choose your anal toys and your anal lubricants carefully. Butt plugs, for example, are specifically design to only go so far, and some anal lubricants contain a little numbing medication to make the backdoor experience a bit easier. Beginners might elect to limit their anal play to a superficial lubricated "rimming" around the anal sphincter.

A couple thoughts before I slide on out of here. Vaseline Jelly has served men well when it comes to self stimulation, but Vaseline should never be used on a woman (since we do not know what grows in that product). Also, being petroleum-based, it should not be used with condoms or latex toys, as it will cause them to deteriorate rapidly. Good sexual lubricants are water-soluble and mix readily with a woman's own lubrication, cleaning up easily after the erotic encounter. Keep your Vaseline for chapped lips!

Lubricants can make anal and vaginal play fun. However, never take a toy, finger or penis from in or around an anus and insert it in or around a vagina. That's a serious 'No, no!' Have separate toys and keep them separate, and to be safe, invest in a sex toy cleaner to kill any bacteria that might decide to hang around.

Some lubricants are packaged so the bottle can be heated in a cup of hot water. The result is a product that is warm and slippery. Aaah, that makes for some fun play not only around the clitoris, but around nipples as well. Try some warm slippery fingers around the sensitive rim on the head of an erect penis. Lubricants make sensual exploration more exciting.

Using an artificial water-soluble lubricant when a condom is in use will decrease the possibility of breakage during intercourse, and here's another prize winning suggestion involving a rubber and a lubricant. Some women are not fond of accepting a man's ejaculate in their mouths at his climax of her oral pleasuring. Here's a tip for such women: Perform your fellatio slowly, adding great variety as you tease the man to a high pitch, stopping short of his point of no return. Squirt several drops of lubricant into the end of a dry condom so when you lay the condom on top of the eager erection, the lubrication will be on the inside. Manually roll the condom down over the head of his penis with your fingers, but then use your mouth to push it down to the base. Now get serious with your blow job, keeping enough pressure on the condom so that it slides with your mouth. The man will experience a warm slippery feeling and we know where that will end. The results of his orgasm will be in the condom, however, and not in your mouth. You can experience the expulsion without worrying about your taste buds, unless of course your guy tastes better than the taste of a latex rubber!

Have fun and stay wet!

Female Sexual Self-Esteem

Volumes have been written on the topics of body-image and on self-esteem, but very little has been said about one important aspect of a woman's self-perception, her sexual self-esteem. This is a delicate topic, but to understand it we are required to look unflinchingly at the psychological and sociological factors that influence a women's concept of her sexual self. At the onset, however, let me first acknowledge two obvious things: First, I am a male (which for some readers will automatically disqualify me as an expert on this topic) and second, many women already have a marvelous sexual self-esteem (and what I will be saying will not apply). With this said, I will risk continuing.

Anatomically, young females see little of their genitals as they look down their bodies. Well known sexuality educator Jessie Potter had remarked that girls have "privates," boys have "publics." Because of female anatomy, I would suggest that for many girls their "privates" were also their "secrets." A female's genitals are not only secret from the world, they often remain secret for many of their owners.

There can be something exciting about having something secret. Mystery and intrigue surround things held secret, but things secret also have a more negative potential. If what is concealed by design and held in private by mandate is also portrayed as bad, anxiety and shame can become associated with it. The socially responsible message to "Just say No" does not help a sexually responsive young woman deal with her erotic desire. If a teenager identifies this natural desire as 'lust' or as 'sin,' she is likely to feel guilty about her sexuality and shameful of that part of her body that seems responsible.

Added to the perception of genitals as bad is the stereotype of a vulva being ugly and smelly. The concept 'dirty' becomes associated with female genitals. A revered physician and sexuality educator, Dr. Mary Calderone, would often remind us that many women have grown up with the bizarre message, "Don't touch yourself down there, it's dirty. Save it for the one you love." One must wonder, if what is down there is so dirty, why would a woman ever want to give it to someone she treasures?

To some extent, the well-intended messages about menstruation can also add to a young woman's sexual self-consciousness. Menstruation is something that must remain hidden. Tampons don't show, pads with wings keep the secret, and mini-pads allow for normal appearing movement. Belts went the way of the bell bottoms, so women no longer have to worry about telltale lines, I wonder how many women grew up thinking they were called 'sanitary pads' because there was something sick or dirty about a very normal process. The cross section of a woman's pelvis in the flier of a tampon box is drawn without a clitoris. A brochure on an enlarged male prostate, benign prostatic hypertrophy, would never show a cross section of a man's pelvis without including a penis. Boys have 'publics," girls have 'privates!'

Overweight women are faced with the challenge of maintaining a good sexual self-image in the face of the media presentation of sexy as the woman with a perfectly proportioned and remarkably firm body. Sex is portrayed as an activity engaged in by this perfect woman and a perfect male partner. Women not fitting this stereotype are disenfranchised by the notion that attracting a sexy young man is the mark of a woman's sexual attractiveness.

There is another problematic notion many women have grown up with, but I think might finally be changing. This is the image of the passive female and the sexually aggressive male whose role is to seduce her. Once seduced, the woman having been turned on by the man is laid in a passive position and mounted, the male orchestrating the coital dance. Many women still in that supine position wonder why they are not reaching orgasm during intercourse, never realizing that the majority of women never do reach orgasm during intercourse and that the missionary position is one of the most *ineffective* ways to attempt to do so. Men in the superior posture act out their image as active, dominant, in control and reliably orgasmic. The women on the bottom remain passive, receptive, to some extent helpless and often wondering "Is that all there is?"

As I stated at the beginning of this article, many women have a wonderfully positive sense of sexual self-esteem, and most of these have probably quit reading this by now. Those of you who are still with me, bear with me a bit longer as I now attempt to offer some tips on improving your sexual self-esteem.

Get your genitals out of the closet. Perhaps doctors and nurses more than any other women have seen genitals with problems. They have not been sensual loving lustful vulvas, they have those that are infected, diseased, or injured. When was the last time you looked at yours, other than wondering about that itch or worried about that discharge. When did you last look and say to yourself, "Neat!" Take a hand mirror and, with ample light, look and say "Hello" to that very special part of your body. Give your vulva a playful nickname! Take pride in your womanhood and remind yourself that there is nothing dirty or ugly or smelly about your body.

It is hard when a woman loses one or both breasts to cancer. Remind yourself that sexuality is not about anatomy, it is about attitude. It's no secret that breasts change their appearance as women age, lots of things begin to sag. Reminisce joyfully about the firmness of your youth. Always value your past without mourning your loss. Stand in front of a mirror and find the angles that are most attractive. Look for the areas that are still sexy.

Take responsibility for your body and for your satisfaction. If you have never masturbated, give yourself permission to try. It really is a very effective way to own your body and your sexuality, not to mention learning what really does work best. If you have a partner, be more active, ask for what you want, and try new things. Have him lay on his back and you mount him. The female superior position is very effective for many women, as they are able to control the movement and get the clitoral stimulation needed for maximum coital pleasure. (Typically this works best when the woman leans forward, stays in tight against her partner, and slides back and forth, rather than sliding up and down.) Take charge, be in control and get what you want. Most men love being "used."

Allow yourself to have sexual fantasies in which you are the pursuer, the seducer. Wear comfortable underwear that helps you feel sexy. Do it for yourself, not for others. Be playful with your little harmless sexual secrets and chase away any old guilt or shame.

Talk to other women about the myth of the passive sexual female. Talk to your partner about your positive sexual attitude. Share your understanding of your own body and what you like and need. Flirt with your partner. Remember, you are a complete sexual being, packaged in a marvelous body and capable of superb sexual experiences, of your choice.

Self-Pleasuring

Traveling Your Pathway Alone

Before taking the big step, if you are comfortable with the idea of self-pleasuring but have not already tried, it is strongly suggest that you learn how to pleasure yourself. Masturbation for women has recently come out of the closet. Self-stimulation is not just for men! Women, of course, have been doing it from the time a female first discovered that her hand could reach her own clitoris, but at some time in history (or *her-story*), female masturbation went underground and was not talked about or condoned in polite society. We now know that good girls do, and it is a valuable means for learning what feels good and what will work. After all, "good girls" have to teach "good boys" what it is they like.

As you get to know your own body and as you give up any embarrassment about how you think you look, smell or taste, it is quite likely that you will become increasingly comfortable talking with your partner about your sexuality. Fortunately, most men are really quite eager to learn what works best for their lover. So, in private, really look carefully and fondly at your genitals, touch yourself, find your clitoris for yourself and allow yourself to discover what feels good. That is what your sexuality is all about – feeling good.

What you learn through self-stimulation can be shared later, but as you touch yourself now, allow yourself to be "selfish," reaping all the pleasure you can from this experience. It is, after all, your body! This is true for both males and females.

Starting Your Trip

Begin with a warm bath and pamper your body. Remember arousing experiences or think erotic thoughts about a special person. Find a place to relax where you feel safe and secure. Light some scented candles, sip a little wine if you choose, and put on some soft relaxing music. You might also begin your sensual self-play with romantic or erotic fantasies, or set the mood by reading from an erotic romance novel. Gradually add in an exploration of the textures of your skin, perhaps as you recall being touched by a loved one.

Do not rush your self exploration. Relax and take time to caress your face, your stomach and your inner thighs. Learn more about your breasts and what feels good. Touch your breasts lightly, but also try a firmer squeeze to find which feels the best. Make circles around your nipples. Pinch your nipples gently (or firmly if you like) and then brush them lightly with your fingers. What works? What feels best? Is one breast more sensitive than the other? Become the expert on your body, for you cannot tell someone what feel best until you discover it yourself.

Moving Along Your Pathway

Place your hand on your pubic bone, feeling the hardness of the bone, padded by soft flesh and covered with your pubic hair. With your palm cupping your pubic bone, let your fingers rest on the large outer lips of your vulva. Press on the bone and make circles, with your fingers moving your entire genital area. You might be able to feel the indirect stimulation of your clitoris with this "massive" movement. If you find that initially you are uncomfortable moving beyond this point, end here. It is good to be able to identify the beginning of anxiety, for it is best to end while still relaxed.

Even after you are comfortable moving into direct clitoral stimulation, start slowly with non-genital caress. If you are dry when ready to move on, use a water-soluble sexual lubricant. As you begin caressing your genitals, focus in on the sensations. It will be counterproductive if you try too hard, so think of this as play, not work! *Remember to stay focused on the pleasurable process of sensual self-exploration without worrying about reaching the goal of arousal or orgasm.*

Continuing On

If you are a male reading this, picture the following in your mind. Imagine you are watching a very special woman beginning to learn more about her sexual anatomy and response.

If you are a female who has never traveled this far before, but are now ready to take the next step in self-stimulation, start here. With fingers slippery from lubrication (artificial or your own), slowly explore the unique intricacies of your genitals. It is better to be too wet than not wet enough. Run a finger gently down the edge of an inner lip, and then down the other side, comparing the sensations. Some women will find that stimulation on one side feels better than on the other. Caress the opening of your vagina, picking up more of your own lubrication that might have collected there. Run your finger up from your vaginal opening, passing up the sensitive valley between the inner lips until reaching the head (or *glans*) of your clitoris. "Flick" your clitoris lightly as you come up from below it. Circle this small sensitive bud to feel the difference. Move up onto the shaft of this sensitive organ, exploring both sides of it.

Experiment with the number of fingers. One might work well for stimulating the tip of your clitoris, but your whole hand might work best for stimulating a broader area. Try two fingers. Try different movements . . . up and down, side to side, and circular. Use different pressures. Try various speeds. It is your body. Be curious and explore.

If you become aroused, you might feel your clitoral shaft become firm. From above, slide two fingers down over your clitoral shaft, one on each side, and stroke up and down. Try circles with your fingers straddling the shaft of your clitoris. When you find what feels best, stay with it, remembering to use the mental imagery that works for you. Anticipate the growing hypertonicity of your muscles as your body responds to the stimulation and erotic thoughts. Go with the flow and allow your body to take over and to react naturally.

Letting Go

If you fear letting go as you feel your arousal building, try to resist any urge to stop. Instead, <u>pretend</u> to have an orgasm. Arch your back, rhythmically squeeze your pelvic floor muscles, thrust with your pelvis, and hold your breath. Then thrash around a bit and moan. *Be wild, be silly, be noisy, be uninhibited and be out of control.* When acting out that pretend-orgasm, exaggerate the outward response. If you practice letting loose during these make-believe orgasms, you will find it happening more naturally. In addition, you will be less likely to feel threatened or embarrassed when opening up with your partner present. So, play some more, try to get into it, and enjoy all the good feelings you can create for yourself. Let yourself go and just let all those feelings unfold.

Quit when you get tired, if you begin feeling sore, get stuck, or have an orgasm. Practice by yourself <u>at least</u> once a week, or at the frequency that works best for you. As with most learning experiences, practice makes perfect. It's your body, so enjoy its full potential for pleasure.

Sexually Out of Sync:
Understanding Levels of Desire

Most sex therapists would agree that of all the problems presented in their offices, the largest category of concerns are those centering around levels of sexual desire. They would also agree that these cases are the most difficult to understand and the hardest to treat. But, let's begin at the beginning and try to understand what sexual desire is and where it comes from.

Sexual Desire Defined

Sexual desire is the internal motivator that signals the biological hunger for arousal and orgasm. In the past it has been called "libido," and today its stirring is commonly known as "getting horny." It is a biological hunger, not too unlike our hunger for food, although no one has ever died from lack of sex. The sexual hunger begins as a subtle yearning and might stay at that level, or it might escalate in intensity and become quite demanding. Following an episode of arousal concluding with orgasmic satisfaction, the level of biological desire decreases. This biological need will, however, resurface in a period of time, this cycle being different for each one of us depending on our biology and our environment. By "our environment" I mean, of course, the amount of sexual stimulation around us, in the form of a desirable and interested partner, exciting visual stimulation, and sensual sounds and aromas.

I'll back up again to point out that there might be confusion in our definition of "sexual desire," for it is often used to identify sexual thoughts, as well as physical urges. I prefer to refer to the former, the sexual thoughts, as "sexual ideation," and reserve the term "sexual desire" for that biological ache that captures a person's attention and wants to direct his or her behavior toward a sexual goal. Thus, someone might honestly say they think about sex, but they have no desire to do it. They might say that their sexual ideation includes memories of wonderful sexual encounters, but there is no physical need to repeat them.

There are those who have positive thoughts about sexuality and a biological sexual need that periodically arises. The satisfaction of a sexual appetite does not automatically require that it be done within the context of a relationship. Some people might abstain from a sexual exchange for reasons relating to their morality or personal values, or just because a suitable partner is not available. Therefore, there are obviously those who respond to their sexual drive with masturbation. Self-pleasuring is an option for one who is waiting or one who is without a partner, and self love should always be practiced without guilt. It is interesting, on the other hand, that there are also those with strong physical needs, but with negative sexual ideation and this prevents them from seeking fulfillment of their sexual appetites, alone or with a partner. Celibacy is a matter of choice, but a lot easier for one who has little or no desire.

Three Types of Sexual Arousal

Let me back up again, for this topic of sexual desire is complex and I need to make another point about arousal. Remember, the physical sexual response cycle begins with desire, which leads to arousal, and, with effective stimulation, culminates in orgasm. There are essentially three types of arousal. First, there is that <u>spontaneous arousal</u> that is closely intertwined with desire and springs up without provocation. The horniness suddenly emerges, closely followed by the physical manifestations of arousal (men get firm, women get wet). This spontaneous arousal is most likely the result of a biological cycle driven by the person's hormonal system, and the most obvious example are the spontaneous erections of the adolescent boy which occur with no external or mental stimulation. The desire and arousal just appear.

With age, other physical changes, and a lot of unknown factors, the incidences of spontaneous arousal diminish. However, there is another avenue to arousal that we can call "psychogenic." The genesis or beginning of the arousal is in the person's psyche or mind, although the biological/hormonal component is still operative. Psychogenic arousal occurs when a person, with positive sexual attitudes and a subtle but growing biological need, begins a sexual fantasy; or sees, hears or smells a desired partner; or sees or reads something erotic or explicit. Psychogenic arousal can be stimulated by a nonsexual touch, a gentle kiss, or some other sensual touch other than on the erogenous areas. We could guess at a percentage and say that the origin of psychogenic arousal is 65% within the mind and 35% within the body. It should be obvious, however, that the percentages can change, but arousal might still occur if the numbers add up to 100.

All is not lost if the percentage of the biological contribution is low. This is when we must rely on nature's backup plan. This we can call neurogenic arousal or reflexogenic arousal, for the pathway to arousal is via a neurological reflex. Remember this avenue, for it is important and I will get back to it.

Sexual Issues Centering Around Desire

Now, let's look specifically at the types of concerns that center around issues of desire. However, I first want to remind the reader that there is no national standard that everyone must meet. If both partners enjoy there mutual sexuality once a month and are both happy about that, there is no problem. If another couple mutually enjoys their sexuality twice a day, seven times a week, and still makes it to work on time, there is no problem. Too often there is a tendency to label someone as "undersexed" or "oversexed" based on some statistic or, more likely, the level of desire of the persons doing the labeling. This is subjective at best, disrespectful at worst.

Each couple must decide what is right for them and, if in agreement, no one should judge their performance. However, a problem might arise if one partner feels the need for sex once a month and the other partner desires it more frequently. This has been called a "desire discrepancy," and can become a major issue in a relationship. I should hasten to add that the old sexist jokes always have the woman saying, "Not tonight," and then claiming the proverbial headache. In reality, a good estimate is that the ratio between women and men is about six to four. That is, out of 10 people with a level of desire lower than their partner's, six will be women. Four of these 10 people will be men.

Issues of desire are further complicated by the fact that newness or novelty are very powerful aphrodisiacs. There might be a lot of spontaneous and psychogenic arousal early in a relationship, but as time goes on, the level of desire diminishes. Although not exclusively, it is often the man who continues to feel the biological desire when time cools what had begun as a passionate relationship. It is recognized that testosterone plays a major role in triggering sexual appetite. Women produce it also, but not in the same quantity as men. So we have issues of familiarity and issues of hormone production, and these are not easily sorted out.

Two Categories of Low Desire

I need to get academic again, forgive me. Low desire might be life-long (chronic) with the person saying, "I never really had a need for sex," or it might be a more recent change and the person reports once having a strong desire but somehow losing interest. With the former, blood chemistry might be involved. With the latter, biological changes (e.g., a pregnancy, menopause, or medication side-effects) might be the culprit, or the introduction of mistrust, disrespect or anger into the relationship could undermine the desire.

Typically, if the lose of desire is related to some physical change, it is "global." That is, the person never feels desire. However, if a decrease or loss of desire has something to do with a change in the relationship or something to do with the partner, it is called "partner-specific." In this case the person feels desire, but is not attracted to their partner. Such a person might report that they are avoiding sex with their partner, but are masturbating on a regular basis.

The Partner's Reaction

Even in a relationship that is otherwise good, partners with a higher sexual interests and drive often have difficulty understanding why their mate is indifferent. All too often they think it is intentional (e.g., withholding sex to punish) or a sign of the loss of love ("If you loved me, you'd want me"). Feelings might be hurt, self-esteem might suffer, and rejection might be perceived when this is not what it is. The one with the higher desire might feel abandoned and undesirable, but the partner with the lower level of sexual drive might be equally bewildered. Not having the appetite, this partner might wonder why their hornier mate has placed so much importance on something that holds so little interest for them. They might feel pressured, could feel guilty, and could even wish they would feel more desire but do not know how to make it happen.

Unfortunately, a chain of events might begin. One partner shows little interest, but tries. The other partner senses disinterest and begins to question. The one with the lower desire could then feel self-conscious and back off. The hornier partner might then lay on a guilt trip. The one with the lower appetite might begin to resent this and shut down even more. The hornier partner might then begin to pressure and the one with less drive becomes angry. This couple is now in serious trouble!

The Place to Start

Let's begin with two first steps that many, many people resist. If the absence or lose of sexual desire is global, the person with the lower sexual appetite should consult a physician and request a complete evaluation of his or her hormone levels. If the absence or lose of libido is partner-specific, it is time to take a good look at the quality of the relationship, both emotional and sexual. Look for anger, resentment, or maybe just boredom! If sex has become mechanical, routine, hurried and one-sided, without a powerful push from hormones, desire will plummet.

People with higher desire than their partners should be aware that the more they push, the more likely it is that their mate will back down. Sexual desire is a natural biological drive and can not be talked, coerced, or shouted into action. The other thing people must learn is to avoid what I have called "all-or-nothing sex." That's when the only time one partner touches the other is when he or she wants physical gratification and does not stop until they get it. There is nothing in-between. This can be particularly devastating to a woman who has low desire for sex but a high need for nonsexual physical affection. Perhaps if she was touched more she would be more willing to try. Men need to remember that for many women, sex is more about the total relationship than about having an orgasm!

It's a Tough Problem

I'll be honest and state that the chances of someone going from zero desire to full steam ahead even with the help of a qualified sex therapist is pretty slim. Hormone supplements might help, but folks should always be aware of any possible side-effects. I do feel, however, that there is a way to deal with a desire discrepancy within the context to a loving and committed relationship if both parties are willing to compromise.

The strategy begins with the couple's mutual agreement to redefine what their sexuality is all about. If one insists sex is only about orgasms, there is going to be trouble! Sexuality must be redefined as the intimate expression of caring, with or without orgasms. It must be viewed as the physical expression of their emotional passion, with or without arousal. This new definition of sexuality should include sensual massage, nonsexual fondling and the verbal exchange of positive thoughts, fantasies and memories.

It must be understood that no one is purposefully rejecting the other, and love still exists even in the absence of frequent and spontaneous arousal. It must also be accepted that strong overwhelming feeling of desire are unlikely, and that this is as much a loss for the one with less desire as it is for the one with the stronger drive. However, it must also be recognized that some compromise must be met if the relationship is going to continue undamaged. It takes two to tango, but the dance is often a slow dance to soft music.

There is Hope

I had written of spontaneous arousal generated by a powerful biological drive. Forget it! I had also written of the influence of the environment in allowing psychogenic arousal, even in the absence of strong desire. To do this, all-or-nothing sex must be avoided. The level of romantic encounters should increase as should the amount of nonsexual touch and loving caress. Turn-ons and turn-offs should be openly discussed, and the couple should reminisce about their past loving and erotic activities together, but without guilt trips.. Communication about pace and timing is essential. Novel and creative activities acceptable to both might be explored to bring some novelty into the bedroom and, in fact, novelty can be added by playing in locations other than the usual room of the house where sexual attempts typically occurred.

Now, all of that probably is something you have read elsewhere. But, the main element in the intimate compromise is to agree to set aside time in advance to relax together and, in a non-pressured atmosphere, to play. Bathing or showering together could be a start. Candlelight and soft music might help set the mood. Nonsexual caress with a warm massage oil would help the relaxation. It might happen that in the sensual process, the desire of the less interested individual might be stirred, and the session might move slowly into sexual activities. The partner with the stronger desire should realize that even if it moves in this direction and even if his or her mate experiences a pleasurable orgasm, the level of spontaneous desire of that partner will not increase. This is a strategy, not a cure!

Focusing on the Process, Not the Goal

In this process that begins almost from ground zero, it is absolutely essential that there is agreement that when one partner says something like "I've gone about as far as I'm going to go," that the other partner will not push. The contribution of the hornier partner to the success of this strategy is his or her agreement to back away from the urge for completion so as not to pressure the other participant. However, the contribution of that partner with the lower desire is the promise to try the next level before asking that the progression end. In other words, if the nonsexual massage feels good and relaxing for a woman with a low sexual appetite, breast stimulation should be tried even in the absence of desire. If that feels good, the next step including genital stimulation might be tried, even in the absence of arousal.

Ignition Problems

Do you remember what I wrote about reflexogenic arousal. It is a neurological reflex that is triggered by direct stimulation of the clitoris of a woman or the penis of a man. With a woman who is not aroused, this should happen only with the added slipperiness of a safe and water-soluble lubricant (like K-Y or Astroglide), or with oral stimulation. There is a chance, if the person without spontaneous desire was able to relax and if the touch was unhurried and in just the right places with just the right timing, that arousal could occur with this direct stimulation of the most erogenous areas. This is what I have called the "jump start" for people with "ignition problems." Many people discover that even though their starters are broken, their motors will run just fine.

But, the jump start might not always occur and so the agreement to back up when something is not working holds true, even when the activities have moved to this level of genital involvement. When a limit is reached, it is very important to back up and slowly back out, even when there has been manual or oral caress of the genitals. However, care should be take to maintain the expression of sensual caring in this "cool down phase." The person with the higher desire can always ask permission to masturbate while their partner holds them, and some partners might even be willing to help. This must never, however, be done to embarrass or intimidate a mate, but rather as the conclusion to an understandable, one-sided, very natural hunger that craves satisfaction.

Desire discrepancies can be troublesome, but with understanding, compassion, and a willingness to risk starting something that might not get finished, partners can avoid the anger and avoidance that might otherwise occur. The physical bonding in a long-term relationship is important enough for couples to seek a compromise that both can live with.

Taking Turns

Most of us already know that men love receiving oral stimulation and probably have been begging for "blow jobs" (fellatio) ever since they first discovered there was more than one opening into which a woman could incorporated a penis. However, turnabout is fair play, and most women, if they give themselves permission, will thoroughly enjoy being on the receiving end of a talented tongue. They will receive this oral stimulation (cunnilingus) with equal or greater enthusiasm than they experience when giving. However, people seem to come in all varieties, and so there are couplings in which the woman loves sucking on her partner's penis, but will not allow herself to be orally stimulated. There are certainly relationships in which the woman loves being "eaten," but refuses to return the oral pleasure. Then there are the men who are pigs when it comes to getting, but adamantly refuse to go down on their partners, and conversely, there are those men who will turn down a blow job, but love orally stimulating their women. People certainly have the right to decide what they want to do and what they want to receive, but within an intimate relationship it is important for both parties to agree on what will and will not be practiced.

I would like to propose to those couples having an interest in oral stimulation that it is important to work together in perfecting the art of both giving and receiving. Open and honest communication is essential, for we are each the expert on our own body and we must, therefore, communicate our unique wants and desires to our partners. Each individual should learn the skills needed to be a good giver, but each must also learn to open up to the full enjoyment of being on the receiver. Men, it seems, are better at being "selfish" in this regard than are some women. With that special partner, a woman needs to learn to enjoy giving the perfect blow job of her choice (and it should be her choice), but she should also learn how to get the most out of receiving her partner's stimulation when he lovingly begins orally stimulating her. It might help a woman to relax and enjoy the oral encounter if she knows that most men truly love arousing a woman and most love doing so orally. Most men love the textures, the aromas, and the tastes associated with cunnilingus. The also love the sounds a woman makes when she is being orally caressed. Trust me on this!

The point I wish to make is that oral sex is best when it is exchanged. It is a loving act that should never become routine or mechanical, and no book should set out to give you a Step A, Step B, Step C set of instructions. Orally pleasuring a special person is too important, to unique, and too intimate to be boiled down to a set of rigid directions. Be playful and experimental. Enjoy your partner, but enjoy yourself as well. Oral sex is much too good to only go in one direction. Some couples, therefore, enjoy simultaneously stimulating each other in a sixty-nine position and this seems to work well for those who can pat their heads and rub their stomachs at the same time.

I would like to suggest, however, that there is also an advantage to taking turns, so that when giving, the giver can joyfully specialize in giving and the receiver can "selfishly" concentrate on the erotic pleasures of receiving. (I hope it is realized that I use the word selfish in a positive way to indicate the willingness to fully enjoy one's own erotic pleasure.) But positions must at some point be exchanged, so that the one had been giving now has their turn to lay back and wallow in the pleasure of this wonderful gift of the oral caress. Simultaneously or taking turns, to orgasmic completion or as foreplay, on a bed or on a table – however you and your partner choose to express your oral intimacy, remember that the most important message I am attempting to communicate is that all of your sexuality should be loving, open, adventurous, and, above all, great fun for both participants!

Some Women Wonder,
"HOW WILL I KNOW IF I'VE HAD MY ORGASM?"

The easy answer to the questions is, "You can't miss it!" While that is probably true, that answer does not help the woman who has never had one or is not sure. Since the orgasmic awareness is such a subjective experience, it might be best to begin at the physical level, and to begin at the beginning.

A Typical Physical Orgasm

Ideally the sexual response begins with a physical hunger. Call it what you will, sexual desire, libido, or horniness. Desire is the yearning between the ears. It is the motivation to seek sexual pleasure and release. The next step in the "sexual response cycle" is arousal. As a woman becomes aroused (turned on), physical changes begin. Blood is sent down into the tissue of her genitals. Her genital lips will swell a bit and might spread open. Her clitoris, (often called the *pleasure bud*) is composed of spongy erectile tissue that engorges, enlarges, and firms. With arousal the clitoris becomes exquisitely sensitive to touch. As the woman responds the muscles around the entrance to her vaginal begin to relax, but the tissue swells a bit and the slippery lubricant seeps out from the opening.

During arousal a woman's nipple might firm. Some will develop a slight rash (call the sexual flush) on their chests. Breathing is likely to change and blood pressure will increase.

With continued stimulation, typically focused on the clitoris, the orgasmic woman will mentally experience her rapidly escalating excitement. Her breathing pattern will change, her psychological awareness will focus on the stimulation, and she will probably close her eyes. As this builds, the typical woman will feel her body begin to tense. The muscles in her legs, pelvis and abdomen will tighten. This is called *hypertonicity* and should not be a reason for a woman to stop! Many women exaggerate this automatic response and consciously tighten the muscles surround their vaginal opening. In fact, a small number of women can orgasm with <u>no</u> external stimulation at all, simply be tightening their abdominal/pelvic muscles. I few have discovered this, much to their surprise, while working out at a health club!

No one quite understands the neurological build up or what the exact orgasmic trigger is (or where it is located). But, the excitement builds to a point that a strong reflex is activated. The muscles in the woman's pelvic floor (called the PC muscles) begin to automatically contract, and the resulting subjective experience of these contractions are the waves of intense pleasure that sweep through her body. Some women will moan, some will cry out, some remain silent. Some women thrust with each contraction and some do not. As the orgasm subsides, some women cry, some laugh, but most just "purr."

I should be quick now to add that if you were to ask twelve orgasmic women to describe their climactic experience, you will get twelve different answers. This may in part be due to slightly different physical reactions, differing types of stimulation, dissimilarity between expectations, and idiosyncratic psychological interpretatons of the event.

Different Physical Responses

During the orgasmic response, as noted above, the muscles of a woman's pelvic floor rhythmically contract. For most women (who have not had hysterectomies) their uterus will also contract, although not in synch with the PC muscles and certainly not with the same intensity. The awareness of these uterine contractions vary among women (and some women might only have been aware of them during a pregnancy). A woman whose awareness is mostly of her pelvic floor contractions will speak primarily of the waves of pleasure. A woman who is mostly aware of her uterine contractions is likely to emphasize a deep feeling of warmth. A woman who experiences a blended orgasm will talk of both the waves and the pleasure deep in her pelvis.

The awareness of the pelvic floor contractions are to some extent dependent on the tonicity of the PC muscle band. The better toned the muscles, the more intense the orgasm. (A chapter on the Kegel Exercise for the PC muscles can be found in this book.)

Different Stimulation

Women are likely to describe a difference in their orgasmic experience depending on the type of stimulation that brought them to their climax – oral, vibrator, manual. Women are likely to describe a difference between reaching orgasm with the manual stimulation by a partner and reaching orgasm with self-pleasuring (masturbation). Women are also likely to report a different experience depending on whether or not there is something (a dildo or a penis) in their vagina. It is sometimes easier for a woman to orgasm with one partner than it is with another, even though she might be unsure of the reason.

Clitoral vs Vaginal Orgasms

It is pretty much accepted that trying to distinguish between clitoral and vaginal orgasms is a confusing and worthless undertaking. If a woman is able (as some are) to reach orgasm with nipple stimulation, should we call this a "nipple orgasm?" And what about the small number of women who can think themselves into a climax. It makes better sense to talk of the location of the orgasmic response, rather than the site of stimulation that triggered it. Above was mentioned the pelvic floor orgasms, the uterine orgasms, and the blended orgasms.

The question of clitoral or vaginal orgasms is really about whether a woman should be able to orgasm during intercourse (or with a dildo). Should a woman be able to orgasm with just vaginal stimulation? It might be nice, but the answer is "No." Can some women orgasm just with vaginal stimulation? The answer is "Yes." Is the G Spot somehow involve? The honest answer is "Maybe, but maybe not." (A chapter on the G Spot follows in this book.) Can the majority of women orgasm with vaginal stimulation alone? The answer is a resounding "No."

A Woman's Expectations

What a woman expects, how she believes she should respond and how she thinks she should act will all impact how she experiences, behaves during, and reports her orgasmic event. A sexual response is a complex blend of many physical and psychological variables.

So how's a woman to act if she is getting close?
    * Be patient
    * Focus stimulation on your clitoris
    * Focus awareness on your clitoris
    * Allow your body to tense
    * Be patient
    * You will feel yourself on the brink of something
    * Be patient
    * You will experience a breaking through phenomena

* Your body will take over and contractions will begin
* You will experience intense waves of pleasure
* The ecstasy will gradually subside
* Your body will relax as you enter the warm afterglow

If you've been there, you know, but might describe the process a bit different. If you have not been there, you will certainly know when you have your first orgasm.

The G Spot

The importance of a woman's clitoris as the source of her greatest sexual pleasure was driven home in the Kinsey studies of the mid-40s, but in 1950, a German obstetrician/gynecologist named Ernst Grafenberg, wrote of a highly sensitive area located <u>inside</u> a woman's vagina. His article appeared in a German medical journal but received little attention by the general public. This erogenous spot had been ignored by writers of sexuality books for lovers until 1982, when the team of Alice Ladas, Beverly Whipple, and John Perry published their book titled ***The G Spot and Other Recent Discoveries about Human Sexuality***. In honor of Dr. Grafenberg, they named the sensitive area "the Grafenberg spot," playfully abbreviating this to simply "the G Spot." This book has never gone out of print and has been translated into nineteen foreign languages.

The area known as the G Spot is located in and up (if the woman is on her back). It can be stimulated by inserting one (or two fingers if this is comfortable for the woman) and bending them up, pushing firmly up into the top of surface the vaginal canal – up behind her pubic bone. Curling the fingers, as though motioning someone to "come here" will then stimulate this area. As many women become aroused, this area begins to swell, increasing from about the size of a pea to perhaps the size of a quarter.

This is an area to explore, but each woman is unique. Some will report pleasurable sensations, some will be indifferent, and some will find it annoying. Since women differ in what they like, a considerate lover will always ask for a woman's feedback when trying something new. Stimulation can then be adjusted to what feels best to her. When next learning about your partner's body, the G Spot area might be an area you will want to playfully (and carefully) explore.

Once more we see the importance of caution, consent and communication.

Communication and Effective Lovemaking

Verbal directions that change the focus of stimulation even a quarter of an inch can mean the difference between a fantastic orgasm and a sleepless night with an unresolved pelvic ache. Those who truly want to satisfy their women should forget all the 'how-to' books and abandon the ego trip of trying to come across as a 'sexpert' (sex expert). Forget all the preferences of previous women in your life or books that you've read, and learn anew from your present partner. Find out what she has learned about her own uniqueness and closely follow her directions. If you give her the lead as she takes her first steps, she'll probably ask you back for more!"

Talking about the wonderful sights, textures, tastes and aromas of your lover must be included in any sex adventure. Verbally, you can talk dirty about animal pleasures or, if preferred, speak delicately of the sensual spiritual moment. Non-verbally, it is great to moan with the pleasure of giving pleasure or to moan in harmony with the sounds of the appreciative receiver of your sensual gift.

Men need to understand that while they are responsive to what they see, women are more responsive to the sounds they hear. It has been said that good sex is noisy. Encourage each other to open up with all forms of expression.

Sexuality without sensuality, touch void of passion and sex simply for the sake of an orgasm follow a primitive hardwired program, but are hollow human experiences. Emotional detachment, fear of intimacy, lack of knowledge, and inability to communicate rob the sexual encounter of its richness. Before beginning to work on mechanical sexual techniques, positions or endurance, perfect your ability to touch your partner in an intimate way; with your hands, with your words and with your heart."

On their own, not all men have figured it out the importance of a woman's clitoris, and many have not heard (or believed) the available information. Some men still need to be educated by the true experts – the women in their lives. In doing so, it is important that a women share information in the best possible way. It is much more enticing and instructive, for example, if she whispers something like "That feels good, but what I like even better is . . . ." Think of the difference between saying, "You're in the wrong spot," versus "That's okay, but it would really feel good if you would move down just a bit." And then the confirmation. "Yes, that's the spot. I love it when you gently rub me there." And then fine tuning, such as, "Little circles are nice."

Men also need to educate the novice woman. If she has never touched an erection before, the man will need to instruct her with words or by guiding her hand with his. Two beginners can have fun learning together, experimenting with touch and giving feedback. Information should be conveyed in a way that does not cause hurt or defensiveness. Be vocal, but in doing so, stay positive. Remember, it is not just what you tell, but how you tell it!

Sexual Fantasies

If you've not had much experience sharing sexual fantasies with a member of the opposite sex, you might not have given much thought to the differences between the typical sexual daydreams of men and those of women? Men, it seems, tend to have more sexual fantasies than women and these are more likely to be paired with masturbation. Men, by nature being visual, are likely to create graphic images of women's sexual bodies and imagine watching them, seducing them or, quite often, being seduced by them. For a male, the storyline of a fantasy is usually quite genital and accompanied with explicit visual images.

Women, in general, fantasize less than their male counterparts. Those women who do fantasize are typically less visual in their sexual daydreams, are usually less focused on genitals, and are more likely to construct a story with the emotional feelings of a romantic encounter. Women also tend to involve more olfactory and auditory memories – memories of smells and sounds. To be sure, however, there are women who masturbate to their fantasies, be they romantic or erotic.

Sexual fantasies can serve many purposes. They can stimulate sexual desire, maintain sexual arousal, enhance the sexual experience, trigger an orgasm and preserve a memory.

The desire to be sexual and the arousal are not something controlled by a switch and easily turned on following the eleven o'clock news. Many people, particularly as they age or as a relationship matures, find that the easy turn ons occur less frequently, particularly late at night. On those occasions when time is limited, fantasies can serve to focus attention on the anticipated erotic event and help induce the desire for sexual intimacy. They can also help ease the anxiety of a beginner.

More than one person has commented, "I'm not able to get excited on a moment's notice. I need time to psych myself up." To induce desire, you can think ahead about what you would like to experience and what you and your partner will give and receive. Imagine the sexual encounter without anxiety, and in your mind let it be an exciting adventure. Recall the good sexual feelings you have experienced while petting or during masturbation, and mentally reminisce about those most memorable past encounters. Conjure up the memory of a partner's warmth, softness, and gentle touch. See your partner's face in your mind's eye and recall that person's sounds of pleasure and the aroma of their hair and skin. Include only the graphic images you are comfortable with.

Desire can be induced mutually throughout the day, with, for example, a phone call to say, "I've been thinking of your wonderful body." The mid-day message, "You won't believe what I want to do to you tonight," might stir the erotic imagination of both partners, causing each to spend the day thinking of the possibilities in store for that night.

For those without a partner, fantasies during the day can become the prelude for an episode of self-loving that evening. Self-stimulation, the normal, natural way of experiencing solitary pleasure, is a healthy outlet for many who are alone. Fantasy during the day can certainly prepare you for the quiet celebration of your own sexual response.

Most of us have had the experience of beginning a sexual encounter, only to find our minds wandering off to the worries of the day or the pressing issues of tomorrow. Erotic fantasy can maintain arousal by pushing away the intrusive nonsexual thoughts. When distractions hit, we need only focus on a pleasant sexual memory or project an exciting visual image on our mental movie screen. Fantasies can be of our current sexual partner, but often they will revolve around persons from the past, coworkers, movie stars, or attractive strangers. Bringing others into fantasies is normal and is justified if it serves the current relationship by eliminating distractions that would otherwise dampen or destroy the passion. Obviously, if someone feels guilty about including others in his or her fantasy script, they should be left out. Some people like a cast of hundreds, while others want to focus exclusively on their current partner.

Many people worry about their fantasies being too "kinky", but such fantasies are really quite common. Unusual fantasies can help maintain arousal and are harmless if there is no compulsion to actually experience an act that would be emotionally or physically harmful to oneself or to others. Whereas honesty is usually the best policy, discretion must be used in the sharing of some unusual fantasies or fantasies involving other people. It is rare that a couple can share such deep, dark, private thoughts without, at best, a little discomfort. Too often the reaction upon hearing a partner's most kinky fantasy is one of jealousy or distrust, if not anger and disgust.

One woman playfully imagined that her partner's penis was enormous, and reported how she would visualize engulfing this gigantic imaginary erection into her body. In her mind she would privately marveled at her vagina's ability to swallow up this massive tool. She quickly acknowledged, however, that she had no desire to experience anything that large in real life, but she did enjoy embellishing her fantasy with the thoughts of dressing this impressive male member in doll's clothing and taking it for walks in the park. During her sexual encounters, this fantasy helped rivet her attention on the pleasure she was feeling from the very adequate, reasonably-size penis of her partner. She was not making a comparison.

One night, this woman decided that it would be fun to share her giant penis fantasy with her partner. To her utter surprise, the man was devastated upon hearing her playful musings! He began worrying that she had been with men who had larger penises than his, fearing that these well-endowed men must have please her more than he could ever hope to do. He erroneously assumed that she could not enjoy his average-size penis, and began to feel totally inadequate as her lover. Fearing he could not satisfy this woman, he backed off sexually. When he did try, he felt self-conscious and, as a result, often failed to become erect. This, of course, led to more avoidance and self-degradation.

In couples therapy this man worked on understanding that his partner's fantasy had nothing to do with his genital size or sexual performance, but made their shared intimacy more exciting for her. In the last therapy session he began laughing and, when questioned, shared his own "pet" fantasy. He had for many years fantasized he was making love to a virgin and that her vagina was the town's tightest. Both agreed that they loved each other, loved the sexuality they shared, and would never again ask about the private fantasies each used to dispel the occasional intruding distractions. The also learned that in reality, tight vaginas and large penises are immaterial when a relationship is based on love and mutual respect.

The consequences of disclosure were more serious for another couple. The man fantasized about having sex with his girlfriend's younger married sister. While he found the sister attractive, he had no illusions about her commitment to her husband and would never, in reality, make a pass at her. When he shared his fantasy, however, his wife expressed anger and disbelief. She became extremely uncomfortable whenever her sister was around and believed that she had to watch them both closely for any signs of subtle flirtation. Angry that she now felt distrustful, not only of her husband, but of her sister as well, she chose to end her relationship with the man rather than further damage her relationship with her sister. The fantasy proved to be too close, too personal, and too threatening.

Many shared fantasies, however, enhance desire and maintain arousal. One night a man entered a singles bar, propped himself up on a bar stool and slowly rotated, carefully surveying the women around him. Apparently no one caught his eye, so he turned his back on the scene and sipped quietly on his drink. About fifteen minutes later, a woman walked in. As her eyes adjusted to the darkened room, she also scrutinized the crowd. She wandered around a bit, being careful not to make eye contact with any of the men scattered around the room. After a few minutes of aimless wandering, she moved up beside the man who was seemingly intent on nursing his drink. Sliding between him and the person sitting next to him, she leaned toward the bar to catch the bartender's attention. As she did, the man felt her breast brush lightly across his arm, but he did not look her way.

After being served, the woman stepped back, drink in hand, and stood behind the man. Aware of her presence, the man turned and looked into her eyes. His unoriginal inquiry, "Do you come her very often?" was met with an abrupt, "No!" As he had turned toward her, his leg had came to rest against her thigh. She made no attempt to avoid the contact, but waited for him to continue his attempt to initiate conversation. Awkwardly he asked, "What do you do for fun?" Both grinned at her response, "I pick up strange men in singles bars." At this point the drink he had been nursing so patiently was gulped down in record time and he asked her to dance. She played at being reluctant, but allowed him to convince her. On the dance floor, they danced as though each was covered by porcupine quills, and a large man on a Harley-Davidson could have driven between them. As they continued to dance, however, they moved closer until, from a distance, it looked as though their bodies had blended into one.

As they left together he asked, "Shall we take your car or mine?" Again giggling, they took his car to the nearest motel, where he produced a bottle of wine from an ice bucket on the back seat. Ralph and Mary, who had been dating for three years, were acting out their shared fantasy. Once in the room, Mary enticed Ralph into seducing her slowly, pretending uncertainty. "I really don't know if I should!" she said coyly as he pretended clumsiness, fumbling to unbutton her blouse and acting bewildered by the complexities of the one-handed unsnapping of a push-up bra.

During their lovemaking, Mary intentionally cried out, "Oh Bill, you make me feel so good," and in the morning, Ralph pretended to have completely forgotten her name. It was a night not soon forgotten, providing the erotic content for many fantasies that followed.

Novelty can get lost in long-term relationships. When a couple becomes comfortable and familiar with each other sexually, they often forget to be romantic. The entire sexual scenario might become routine, taking place at the same time of the day, in the same location, and all too often in a hurry to completion. While it might be impractical for most of us to make love on a beach, in fantasy we can imagine the sound of the ocean, the warmth of the sand beneath our body, and the excitement of making love under the stars. Perhaps yours will be a fantasy of making love in the woods, or in an old barn, or in the backseat of a car you had as a teenager. You can pick the spot, for you are the casting and scenery director.

Some fantasies can be acted out, e.g., a pick up in a grocery store. But most fantasies are just private thoughts that need not have a complex storyline, or a large cast of characters. Working too hard at building a sexual fantasy can become a distraction, defeating one of its purposes. The best fantasies are often quite simple and tied in with pleasant memories. Often it is visual, creating a mental image of a part of the partner's body that is pleasing to look at, but impossible to see in the dark or in a particular position. At times words can be added to the fantasy while forming the mental image "I love looking at your sweet buns."

Special fantasies can be saved for those times when an orgasm is a bit elusive. These favorites can often add the final bit of excitement needed to trigger a powerful climax. Search your inventory of fantasies. Is there one that is particularly powerful? Is there a favorite that is best saved for the climax? If you discover that you have a *trigger fantasy*, use it sparingly so as not to wear it out. When you are close to orgasm and hovering on the brink, call up that trigger. These powerful pet fantasies are best kept secret.

It is nice in the afterglow of a loving and lustful encounter, even without intercourse, to snuggle together and reminisce. Images of the encounter can then be stored for later retrieval to induce desire, maintain arousal, or even trigger an orgasm. Fantasies serve many functions from getting started to getting finished. Remember, sexual fantasies before, during and after a sexual encounter are normal, natural and often helpful in changing a routine experience into a new and exciting event.

About the Author

Robert W. Birch, Ph.D., certified sexologist and adult sexuality educator, is now retired, but had maintained anindependent psychological practice, specializing in marital, family and sex therapy for well over 35 years. Dr. Birch received his Bachelors Degree from Muskingum College in 1960, his Masters Degree from the Ohio University in 1962, and his Ph.D. from the University of Wisconsin in 1967.

He has been a sex therapy consultant to the Medical Center at Wright-Patterson Air Force Base, has been an adjunct faculty member in the Ohio University Psychology Department and in the Ohio State University Family Therapy program. Dr. Birch has served on the national board of directors of the American Association for Marriage and Family Therapy (AAMFT), the American Association of Sex Educators, Counselors and Therapists (AASECT), and the Board of Examiners of the American Board of Family Psychology.

Dr. Birch was the first Certified Sex Therapist in the State of Ohio. Before his retirement, he had been certified by AASECT as a Sex Therapist, Sex Educator and Supervisor and was a Clinical Member, Fellow and Approved Supervisor of AAMFT. He was certified as a Family Therapist by the National Alliance of Certified Family Therapists, and was certified as a Sex Therapist and Supervisor by the American Board of Sexology.

He was a Founding Fellow of the American Academy of Clinical Sexologists, a Fellow of the American Academy of Family Psychology, and a Diplomate of the American Board of

Family Psychology. He holds a lifetime certification as Sexologist by the American College of Sexologists.

Dr. Birch has presented over 350 guest lectures and lead over 100 professional workshops and seminars. He has served as the Audio-Visual Review Editor of the *Journal of Sex Education and Therapy* as well as being on the Editorial Board of that journal and of the *Journal of Family Therapy*. He is the coauthor of a chapter on Female Sexual Concerns in a book titled *Twenty Common Health Concerns of Women*. He had been a regular guest on radio and TV and continues to be interviewed for national magazines.

Dr. Birch believes that our sexuality is a gift to be enjoyed by consenting adults in loving ways, but never taken too seriously, lest we forget that sex is supposed to be fun. In his retirement he has moved to rural Ohio where he continues to write (with wisdom and wit) in the company of his wife Susan, four dogs, two cats and a very spoiled cockatiel named George.

OTHER SEXUALITY
SELF-HELP BOOKS BY THE AUTHOR

ORAL CARESS: The Loving Guide to Exciting a Woman
1-57074-307-X, 1996

CUNNILINGUS: Warm Her Heart and Tickle Her Pink
1-57074-500-5, 2006

A SEX THERAPIST'S MANUAL: Resources for Clinical or Educational Use 1-57074-320-7, 1996

MALE SEXUAL ENDURANCE: A Man's Book about Ejaculatory Control 1-57074-349-5, 1997

SENSUAL PATHWAYS TO PLEASURE: A Woman's Journey to Orgasm, Coauthored by Cynthia Lief Ruberg, 0-55703-823-5, 2006

SEX *AND THE AGING MALE: Understanding and Coping with Change* 1-57074-482-3, 2000

A SHORT BOOK ABOUT LASTING LONGER: Step by Step Basics for the Management of Premature Ejaculation 1-57074-486-6, 2001

WHAT I KNOW ABOUT SEX: Problems and Pleasures
1-45152-862-0, 2010

These books are available from the author's website at www.oralcaress.com or on Amazon.com.